Super Presti

West Ridi

West Riding Automobile Co. Ltd

David W Allen

Cover: **SHL 873** (**873**), a 1961 Guy Wulfrunian/Roe and one of the early deliveries of the type, makes its way out of Wakefield along Lower Westgate on a local service. *(John Banks Collection)*

Rear cover: **JHL 983** (**803**), a 1957 AEC Reliance with Roe Dalesman coachwork: a classic design in its day. West Riding's fleet of five gave up to 10 years service and one is now preserved. *(Keith Watson)*

Title page: **HL 8623** (**525**) was a 1938 Leyland TS8c with Roe bodywork. It was one of a number of single deckers, known as "band buses", fitted with roof racks principally for the many brass band hires in the district. 525 lost its rack in 1949 when reconditioned and survived in service into 1957. *(Senior Transport Archive)*

Opposite page: **HL 5325** (**20**), one of the original tram replacement buses, was a Roe-bodied Leyland TD2 dating from 1932. It is seen against the backdrop of Leeds Corn Exchange in its early years still sporting the "bow-tie" motif and, no doubt, its original petrol engine. *(John Banks Collection)*

Below: **HL 5224** (**338**) was the first of ten similar 32-seater Roe-bodied Leyland LT3 Lions delivered in 1931: the start of a long association with both suppliers. *(John Banks Collection)*

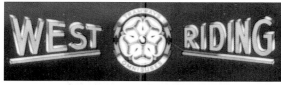

TELEGRAMS { TRAMWAYS OFFICE; WAKEFIELD.
{ TRAMWAYS DEPOT; CASTLEFORD.

Yorkshire (West Riding) Electric Tramways Company,
Limited.

CENTRAL OFFICE *Belle Isle.*

TELEPHONE 213. WAKEFIELD.
" 17. CASTLEFORD.

Wakefield mon. 11th Dec. 1922.

MOTOR DEPARTMENT

MOTOR COACH SERVICES TO ALL PARTS.   SOLE WEST RIDING AGENTS FOR
SPECIALIST REPAIRERS TO COMMERCIAL VEHICLES.   BRISTOL COMMERCIAL VEHICLES.

GARAGES AT WAKEFIELD AND CASTLEFORD ALWAYS OPEN.

INTRODUCTION

Fast receding are the days when the familiar buses of the West Riding Automobile Company Ltd, J Bullock and Sons (1928) Ltd (B & S) and South Yorkshire Road Transport Ltd could be seen on the highways and byways of the coal-mining districts of the old West Riding of Yorkshire and further eastwards into the Vale of York.

In the case of Bullock's B & S Motor Services, it is over 50 years since they were last seen and absorbed by West Riding, followed by South Yorkshire in the 1990s.

The final operating territory covered by the three companies stretched from Bradford in the West through Leeds to York and Goole in the East; southwards the area spread through Wakefield and Barnsley to Sheffield and Doncaster. All three companies had liveries that were bright and yet very different: West Riding chose green and cream with red wheels for their main fleet, though buses used on the ex-tramway routes retained the red and cream of the former trams for a number of years; B & S chose maroon and red; South Yorkshire retained two shades of blue, both having cream relief bands. The three companies shared the same territorial area and their roots and development were somewhat intertwined.

The West Riding Automobile Company Ltd stemmed from tramway operations originally set up by national and local business men in the Castleford and Wakefield districts. These two places were to remain the only bases during the major expansion of West Riding's original bus operations in the first 30 years of its existence. It sold out to the National Bus Company in 1967, before reverting back to independence in 1987, and eventually becoming part of the Arriva Group.

J Bullock and Sons (1928) Ltd (B & S), however, was the first of the three to commence bus operations, from a base in Featherstone where the original founder Jim Bullock had a grocery shop. Other bases were soon formed as services expanded in the Wakefield, Normanton, Selby and Doncaster areas. Jim Bullock's five sons branched out into various forms of transport including removals. Of the bus companies, B & S was the first of the three to lose its independence and identity, being bought out by its main rival, West Riding, in 1950 after a number of earlier takeover attempts had failed.

South Yorkshire Road Transport Ltd was formed after a split in the Bullock family, when Ernest Bullock left B & S in 1929 and acquired the South Yorkshire Motor company in Pontefract, then in financial difficulties, and renamed it South Yorkshire Motors Ltd. This small South Yorkshire company outlived its 'parent' by nearly 45 years. South Yorkshire Road Transport Ltd, as it finally became, had been absorbed by the Arriva Group along with West Riding Automobile by 1998.

It is hoped that the pages of this first book will give an insight into the varied history of the largest and final survivor of these three Yorkshire companies, West Riding Automobile Company Ltd, which spanned nearly a century, with a particular reminder of the many and various new vehicle-types that passed through the company's hands.

THE WEST RIDING AUTOMOBILE COMPANY LTD

1904 and the early years

The West Riding Automobile Company, like some other long established bus companies, developed from tramway systems set up at the turn of the last century. Indeed, West Riding's roots and routes can be traced back to the Wakefield City and District Omnibus Company Ltd, which operated double-deck horse buses in the 1890s; or more specifically to the Wakefield and District Light Railway Company, which commenced tramway operations in August 1904 on routes serving Agbrigg-Wakefield-Ossett, and Sandal-Wakefield-Stourton (Leeds) to connect with the Leeds Corporation system, and a branch to Rothwell which were to become the red bus routes when the trams were finally abandoned in 1932.

The Yorkshire (West Riding) Electric Tramways Company was established in 1905 to acquire control of the Wakefield company and the operation of trams on the new Normanton-Castleford-Pontefract tramway section built by the United Tramway Light Railway and Electric Syndicate and opened in October 1906. A total of 24 miles of track was operated on the two systems, which were never linked.

Further systems had been planned and authorised to extend the Pontefract line to Knottingley, Normanton to Wakefield via Altofts and Stanley Ferry. But railway opposition to plans to extend the system from Castleford to link with the Rothwell line via Methley and Oulton precluded any further development of the two operational systems. An in-depth account of the Tramways of Dewsbury and Wakefield can be obtained from the 1980 book of that title by W Pickles.

In 1908 the first approach was made to the tramways company to run a motor bus service from Crigglestone to Wakefield, but it was not considered viable. By 1913, future tramway system plans had, however, been abandoned and serious consideration was given to operating motor bus services from Wakefield to Alverthorpe and Ardsley within an initial plan. This was followed by a comprehensive scheme to provide bus services to a wider district around Wakefield. With this in mind, buses had in fact been ordered from the Daimler company in 1914, but the First World War stopped further progress.

The advent of the motor bus, and track maintenance problems after the First World War, prompted the tramway company to again reappraise its operational policy. These problems were further aggravated by the prolonged miners' strike in 1921, which brought severe traffic losses, the movement of miners being one of the principal sources of the company's revenue.

It had become clear that the existing tramway network could not be viably extended. The first of the two systems, Normanton-Castleford-Pontefract, was closed down in November 1925. The other Wakefield system, as already mentioned, ceased operations in May 1932.

Harry England, who had managed the tramway operations and became West Riding's Managing Director in 1922, was a leading and respected figure in the original formation of the Tramways and Light Railways Association. He was also a Director of the Lancashire United Transport and Power Company and the South Lancashire Tramways Company. Hence the bus operator Lancashire United Transport (LUT) began to develop on similar lines to the West Riding red fleet with a not dissimilar livery showing the familiar garter band on the rear of vehicles. Both companies enjoyed a long period of friendly rivalry as to which of them was the largest independent bus operator in the country.

In 1921, it was agreed that some £30,000 should be invested in a bus fleet: a large amount for a provincial company at that time. This heavy investment reflected the foresight of the company's management, which helped to repel the numerous small and short-lived operators who were making incursions into the West Riding's territory. Sound route planning was complemented by rational fare stages, stopping points and timetabling of journeys.

Consequently, in 1922 a fleet of 22 normal-control 4-ton Bristol chassis with 30-seat bodies built by Bristol began to arrive. Most of

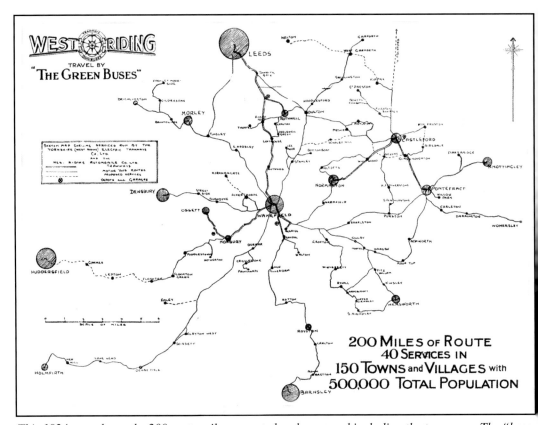

This 1924 map shows the 200 route miles operated and proposed including the tramways. The "bow-tie" motif was also devised at this time and applied to both trams and buses.

this initial order, whose fleet numbers commenced at 101, had dual doors. This was quickly followed in 1923 by a further 16 similar chassis with Strachan and Brown bodies. The next three years brought a further 100 Bristols into the fleet including 20-seaters on 2-ton chassis with Bristol full-fronted bodywork giving a rather racy appearance. West Riding showed an astonishing policy of standardisation for an independent bus company at that time. The choice of Bristols seems to have been a wise one: some of the vehicles lasted in service for eleven years, somewhat exceptional at that stage of bus development.

Other fledgling companies in the area were purchasing Leylands, Albions, Daimlers, Lancias, etc.; few were buying Bristols. This streak of independence was to show itself in later years as it defied the temptation to join the large groupings being formed in the industry.

The bus services officially commenced operation on Easter Monday 1922 from the

established tram depots at Belle Isle, Wakefield and Wheldon Road, Castleford.

However, the first services had been advertised to commence on 6th February 1922, offering three services a day in each direction, weekdays only, between Wakefield and Crigglestone via Thornes, and Wakefield to Morley via Ardsley. Other areas around Wakefield and Castleford quickly gained services including Leeds, Pontefract, Knottingley and villages en route. By the end of 1923 some 20 services were operating in the Wakefield area alone. In Castleford the first buses started to shadow the tram routes to deflect competition from the independent operators who were springing up, West Riding at the same time assessing likely traffic growth.

On 16th November 1923, The West Riding Automobile Company was registered as the motor bus operating subsidiary of the tramway company. This subsidiary company was formerly wound up on 30th June 1935 but reappeared the following day with the assets

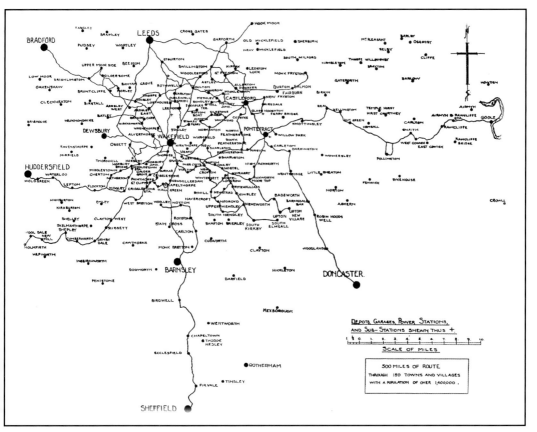

The route map of 1930 shows an expanded route system of 500 miles.

and official name exchanged with 'The Yorkshire (West Riding) Electric Tramways Co Ltd' as a legal requirement.

In 1924 West Riding commenced services into Leeds from various points of its operating region. This was not without constant pressure on Leeds Corporation along with other operators for the necessary licences. In Bradford, the company was initially denied rights to enter the city by the Corporation on a route through Drighlington. It appealed to the Ministry of Transport in a test case affecting many other similar applications in other towns. In 1926 the High Court ruled against the Corporation allowing West Riding and other independent bus companies into the city.

Such was the planned expansion of the bus business that a new garage was built adjacent to the tram sheds at Belle Isle; it housed 40 buses and was officially opened by the Mayor of Wakefield in December 1922. About the same time, a smaller building was erected in Wheldon Road, Castleford, adjacent to the tram

sheds for the same purpose. In 1926 West Riding ceased producing its own electricity for its tramway operations and refurbished the Belle Isle premises to provide further facilities for its growing bus fleet. Garage accommodation was further increased in 1936 as the Leyland Tigers and Titans arrived. Castleford and Wakefield were to remain the only operating bases until 1950.

1930 - Growth and Consolidation

The Road Traffic Act (1930) brought regulation and order to the haphazard way the industry was developing. West Riding immediately applied for licences covering the 99 services it was operating. Under this Act, the railway companies obtained powers to invest in the larger bus companies and groupings that had been established during the formative years of the 1920s and early 1930s. In 1931 West Riding declined a suggested joint-working agreement with the LNE and LMS railway companies.

This was the style of timetable, shown actual size, that was published throughout the 1930s.

They also avoided the acquisitional activities of the groups: Thomas Tilling, British Electric Traction (BET) and British Automobile Traction, which had acquired or were acquiring control of the major companies surrounding West Riding's territory, including the West Yorkshire Road Car Co. Ltd (Harrogate), East Yorkshire Motor Services Ltd (Hull), Yorkshire Traction Ltd (Barnsley) and Yorkshire Woollen District Transport Ltd (Dewsbury). West Riding managed to remain independent for a further 35 years.

West Riding's purchasing policy was to change in 1930 when their allegiance changed to the Leyland chassis which was leading the way in bus development. The last batch of Bristol BGW (4-ton) 30-seat single-deckers came in 1931. A 1924 example is preserved. The first Leylands appeared in 1927 in the form of Lion PLSC1s followed by Titan TD1s and Lion LT2s; bodies, both single- and double-

deck, came initially from Leyland and then Charles H Roe, of Leeds. The first double-deckers had open staircases.

Further single- and double-deck vehicles came on Leyland LT, TDc and TSc chassis; there were also three Leyland KPZ2 Cub 24-seat buses, one of which is also preserved. By the early 1930s, the fleet had grown to 200 and the route mileage to over 500. Nearly all the chassis obtained during this period for the green fleet were fitted with torque-convertors, which was unusual for a non-municipal operator. West Riding was to become the largest company operator of this transmission: 'Gearless Bus', as it was known and usually identified on the radiator grille. Heavy fuel consumption, poor hill-climbing and handling difficulties in snow and ice conditions led to these transmissions being replaced by orthodox manual gearboxes in the postwar period.

In 1936 the first double deck low-height bodies, produced by Roe with an elegant curved profile, were fitted to a batch of Leyland Titan TD4c chassis for the green fleet; this Roe design became common in the West Riding fleet, as it did in many another. They had an unusual arrangement on the top deck: seat rows alternated between 4 and 3 seats per row, giving an extra degree of comfort but a total capacity of only 48 seats.

In the same period a large delivery of Leyland single-deck Tiger TS7c chassis commenced. The first batch, which arrived in 1935, had Leyland bodies and were used as ambulances during the Second World War. Most of these received new Roe bodies after the war. Further deliveries carried the new-style Roe single-deck composite body. Further batches of Tiger TS8c models included some with deep, roof-mounted luggage carriers, used for the transport of instruments on the numerous brass band private hires in the Company's area.

By this time one could have been forgiven for thinking that West Riding was just another

BET subsidiary with a highly standardised Leyland fleet with Roe BET style bodies.

Many of these prewar Leyland TDs, and the TSs in particular, had exceptionally long lives with the last examples being withdrawn in the early 1960s. Twenty-five years of service was not unknown. Indeed, one single decker (fleet No. 407) lasted 31 years - the last 3 as a garage towing vehicle at Selby depot, with a similar one based at Castleford depot. This Leyland only policy was to remain for the next 10 years with the exception of two Guy Arabs obtained for the red fleet.

As far as the tramway replacement fleet was concerned - the red fleet - 50 buses were ordered in 1932/3 to replace the Wakefield-based system's trams; they were painted red as the trams had once been. Apart from the two Guy Arabs, they were rugged Leyland Titan TD2s initially fitted with petrol engines, thus following the Leyland sales slogan of the day, "When you bury a tram - mark the spot with a Titan"! They had distinctive 48-seat Roe highbridge centre-entrance bodies with twin staircases. A further five TD4cs joined the red fleet in 1936, this time fitted with the torque convertor transmission - a useful aid for such multi-stop services - and the new-profile Roe body. The fleet numbers of the red buses commenced at 1 and eventually ran through to the second generation AEC Regent IIIs which finished at 117.

In 1927 West Riding, along with Barnsley and District Traction (shortly to become Yorkshire Traction Ltd) and Yorkshire Woollen District (both BET companies), purchased County Motors (Lepton) Ltd, of Huddersfield. County operated as a separate small subsidiary for a further 50 years.

During the early thirties seven small bus companies were absorbed, mostly within a ten-mile radius of Wakefield, adding almost 40 buses of various makes to the fleet. The largest of these undertakings were J Richard Fox (Junior), and Newton and Ward, both of Rothwell; and Hartley Brothers, and Rhodes of Kippax, in 1933 and 1934 respectively, adding 20 buses to the fleet. Negotiations had also taken place with West Riding's biggest rival, Bullock, but nothing materialised at this time.

By the mid 1930s West Riding's compact operating territory had reached maturity in an area roughly bounded by Barnsley, Holmfirth, Huddersfield, Bradford, Leeds, Castleford, Knottingley and Doncaster, with spurs to Goole, Selby and Sheffield. Joint services to Sheffield developed early with Yorkshire Traction and the Sheffield Joint Omnibus Committee, and other, shorter, routes were shared with Yorkshire Woollen.

Up to the 1930s, the Bell Punch ticket machine as used by the trams was retained. West Riding then began to use the TIM ticket machine in various types until the common 'Ultimate' came into use from the early 1950s. TIM machines came back into use in 1963 in particular for the one-man-operated buses. In 1981 Almex ticket machines were being used for one-man-operations and TIM for conductor-operated services. By 1993 'Wayfarer' computerised ticket machines were in full use at all depots, replacing all previous types.

1940 - A period of change

When the threat of war loomed in 1939, the 1935 Leyland TS7c vehicles were converted to ambulances with perimeter seating; they were used for meeting trains and conveying stretcher cases to local hospitals. These and other single deckers were hired to local military units and some sent to Hull and Sheffield to assist the blitzed cities in bringing back casualties to the specialist burns unit at Pinderfields Hospital, Wakefield. Double-deckers were lent to London and Sheffield.

At the same time, West Riding was also placing orders for 60 new buses, still with their erstwhile suppliers Leyland and Roe. Most of these orders were originally planned to replace the red fleet. In the event, only a handful of 'unfrozen' (chassis that had been in build, or built from parts already in stock, when war broke out) double deck Leyland TD7s were released by the Ministry of Supply to Roe and completed for the green fleet before 'prewar' production ceased during 1941. One TD7 chassis was diverted from Roe by the Ministry of Supply to Park Royal to form the basis for a prototype 'utility' body; the latter entered service with London Transport as STD101. West Riding managed through the Ministry of War Transport to obtain the balance of the order

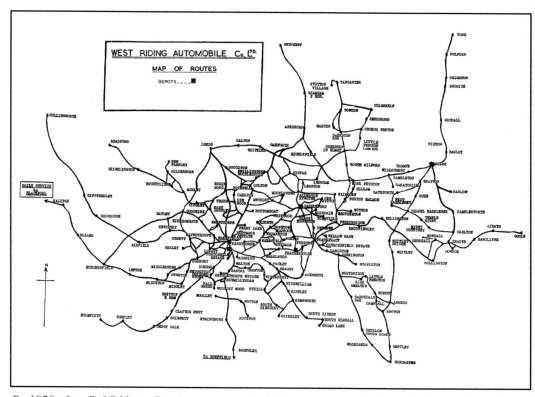

By 1950 when B &S Motor Services was acquired, the route system had reached its zenith as shown.

from Guy with Arab I and II chassis and even to retain their preferred body builder - Roe, who provided the 'utility' and 'relaxed utility' low-height bodies for the green fleet. A few of the Guys arrived in red fleet livery, but eventually were repainted green. West Riding took the last 'relaxed utility' body manufactured by Roe in January 1946 on a Guy Arab (fleet No. 618). Many of the Guys were refurbished or rebuilt in the early 1950s; some survived into the mid 1960s, giving long and reliable service in all parts of the Company's territory.

Apart from the last Guy Arabs, the first new postwar vehicles appeared in the form of AEC Regent IIIs with Roe centre-entrance bodies, which replaced the Leyland TD2s in the red fleet. The first nine chassis (56 to 64) were of the London Transport RT type, of which a number were obtained by a few other companies and municipal operators in the north, being referred to as 'Provincial RTs'. A shortage of bodybuilding capacity for London Transport requirements allowed these badly needed chassis to be released to provincial

operators. By 1949 the entire red fleet had been replaced with the AEC Regents, a few eventually joining the green fleet later in their lives.

New buses were difficult to obtain at this period and much rebodying and renovation work was carried out internally by the company and by external bodybuilders, particularly on the utility Guy Arab double-deckers. Most of the Leyland TS7s used as ambulances during the War received new Roe bodies. At the same time, two TS7s transferred from the County fleet were rebodied and reregistered (Nos 678/9).

The first of a large fleet of all-Leyland double-deck Titan PD2s for the green fleet arrived in 1948, 75 being delivered up to 1950; 16 were highbridge vehicles, the first in the green fleet, which were chiefly for the longer routes not restricted by low bridges. The buses replaced at this time included many of the prewar Leyland TD4, TD5 and TD7 Titans. About 20 West Riding disposals, mostly double-deckers, eventually found their way to Barton Transport Ltd, of Chilwell,

Nottinghamshire, another large independent company. The Leyland TD7s had been in service with West Riding for only ten years and gave up to another ten with their new owners; others were rebuilt giving a similar length of service. Presumably, West Riding had a surplus of double-deckers at this time. Small batches of AEC Regal III single-deckers with Roe bodies were also delivered during this period.

In May 1950, negotiations with the British Transport Commission for a possible sell-out failed. Sir Ronald Leon, the Chairman of West Riding, indicated that a price could not be agreed and, furthermore, he felt that the future of the road passenger industry under the recent Transport Act seemed very obscure.

However, in September that year West Riding finally reached an agreement to 'amalgamate' with the Company's major rival, J Bullock and Sons (B & S Motor Services), at a cost of some £500,000. One hundred and seventy buses, together with depots in Wakefield (2), Featherstone, Selby and Doncaster, were taken over. (The Bullock buses will be described in detail in a further book.) This increased the West Riding fleet to more than 400 units, with an approximate depot allocation as follows: Belle Isle (Wakefield) 190 vehicles, Savile Street (Wakefield) 50, Castleford 100, Featherstone 50, Selby 35 and Doncaster 6.

West Riding had unequivocally become the largest independent bus company in the country. Its operating area spread eastwards into the Selby (to which town West Riding's own services had ceased in the 1930s), York and Doncaster areas. It also included the all-year-round express service from Wakefield to Blackpool, the first long-distance express service to be operated by West Riding, and the seasonal weekend services to the East Coast.

It was a near perfect amalgamation with the small Doncaster depot of Bullock's being the only major casualty. Even the existing fleet numbers fell into place: B & S between 130 and 345 and West Riding between 50 and 120 (red fleet), and 400 and 700 (green fleet). Within days of the take over, two Leyland TS7 single-deckers were despatched to Selby (Nos 487 and 497) followed some weeks later by six green highbridge Leyland PD2 Titans (Nos 654/6-8/61/2) which gave a greater degree of comfort

on the longer routes operated from this depot, Leeds-Selby-Goole and York-Selby-Doncaster; the Titans replaced B & S lowbridge Leyland TD5 and utility Daimler CWA vehicles. By late 1964 the entire batch of 16 green highbridge buses was operating from Selby.

The astonishing assortment of vehicles - all purchased new - inherited from B & S, to be absorbed into a highly standardised West Riding fleet, included AEC, Bedford, Daimler, Guy, Leyland and Seddon chassis. Bodies were from an even more varied list, including Barnaby, Brush, Duple, Hindle, Longford, Mulliner, NCME, Roberts, Roe, Strachan and Willowbrook; there were also rebuilds from Bullock's own body shop in Wakefield. Double-deckers were all low-height. Some outstanding Bullock orders for all-Leyland PD2 double-deckers and further Seddon single-deckers arrived shortly after the take-over.

An AEC Regal IV with Roe bodywork (No. 706) - West Riding's first underfloor-engined bus - was exhibited at the 1950 Commercial Motor Show at Earls Court on the Roe stand. It had a narrow entrance, did not find favour with West Riding and was not placed in service. However, a similar vehicle with centre entrance was obtained in 1951 (No. 709).

In 1952, Major Eastwood, Chairman of the Yorkshire Area Traffic Commissioners, officially opened West Riding's own much-needed bus station in Wakefield, that had cost some £60,000 and which relieved much street parking of buses in various parts of the city.

The same year saw Roe bodied Leyland PS Tiger coaches (Nos 720-5) and buses (Nos 726 -37) added to the fleet; these were the last half cab single deckers to be purchased and one has been preserved. These somewhat low-height buses were able to access pit yards where there was a height problem for the taller underfloor-engined buses. There was a break in the flow of Leyland products during this period when a batch of ten Roe-bodied AEC Regent III double-deckers was placed in service. During 1953 there was a further delivery of all-Leyland PD2s. The first four (Nos 739-42) were painted in red, white and blue for Coronation Year; the destination indicated 'Prosperity via Peace'. These buses were placed at various depots and gave free rides over Coronation Week.

In 1954 the first concealed-radiator double-deckers arrived, on the Leyland PD2/22 chassis (Nos 752-61). The blank area at the top of the 'tin front' marked the location planned for Midland Red's BMMO logo, that operator having taken the first orders of this design. All further traditional double-deckers had concealed radiators.

In 1955, a surprise change of policy produced 25 Guy Arab IVs with Roe bodies (Nos 762-86) followed by 45 more over the next two years, all fitted with rear platform doors for the longer distance services. A number of Roe-bodied AEC Reliance single-deckers (Nos 799 - 817) was also purchased in bus and coach form with underfloor engines, allowing a significant increase in seating capacity over earlier half-cab designs. In 1956, with a shortage of double-deck capacity, West Riding took an unusual step in rebodying 12 Leyland PS1 single deck buses (ex-B & S) with Roe double-deck bodies, which retained their original registration numbers but gained new fleet numbers (787-98). In December 1956 the terminus of the West Riding red services, Wakefield-Kettlethorpe, and Rothwell, moved from the original tram terminus at the Corn Exchange, Leeds, to a small purpose-built bus station in Cross York Street; it remained there until March 1969 before transferring to the Central Bus Station, from where most of the green fleet and other companies operated.

1959 - The Wulfrunian era

West Riding's Chief Engineer, Ronald Brooke, had an idea for a low-height 30ft-long maximum-capacity double-deck bus, and in 1957 the Company approached Guy Motors about building it. There had already been discussions with AEC but little interest was shown; an AEC Bridgemaster demonstrator (76 MME), however, was used for two months in 1958, mostly on the red routes.

A close relationship began with Guy to develop the somewhat revolutionary double-deck bus, the Wulfrunian: a 75-seater that retained the engine at the front as well as the entrance, a design that opposed the new rear-engined Leyland Atlantean. A prototype arrived in 1959 (No. 863) and deliveries were made over the next five years totalling 126 buses.

Initially, the allocation was split between the red and green fleets, but eventually they all became green, when there was no longer any requirement to differentiate the old tramway routes. Only 137 Wulfrunians were ever built of which 132 eventually came into the West Riding fleet; these included two from the jointly owned County Motors (Lepton) Ltd, one each from West Wales and LUT; two Guy ex-demonstrators in Wolverhampton Wanderers colours provided spares for the fleet. One of these rare vehicles is preserved in running condition.

Reliability problems and high maintenance costs, particularly with the revolutionary front suspension system and disc brakes, led to their early withdrawal from service. During their life, overall weight had to be reduced by removing seats to alleviate these problems. All the Wulfrunians were withdrawn well within the first half of their planned lifespan. The final buses had seating capacity reduced to 67. Guy Motors, by then, were suffering from declining sales and were not in a position to resource the expenditure required to rectify the technical design problems of the Wulfrunian. Guy went into receivership in 1961 and was acquired by Jaguar Cars Ltd, the owners of Daimler.

It therefore came as little surprise to see a Leyland Atlantean on demonstration in March 1964 followed by a Daimler Fleetline in September 1965.

In May 1961 George Henry Margrave, the long-serving Managing Director of West Riding, who had taken over from Harry England, retired. He had been with the Company for 41 years, 35 of them at the helm, and had seen the final transitional days from tram to bus. Herman Scott took over as a Director and General Manager some time later. In October 1964 a local man, Harry Watson, became Chairman of the Company in succession to Sir Ronald Leon. Watson had been a board member since 1947.

September 1961 saw the commencement of one-man bus operation from Belle Isle and Selby depots. A fleet of Roe-bodied AEC Reliance dual-doorway single-deckers (Nos 920-31) were purchased for this development. As one-man operation extended over the next few years, further single deckers were re-equipped. From the late 1960s, the Atlantean and Fleetline double-deckers eventually went back to Roe for periscopes to be fitted for this purpose.

In August 1963 the small ex-B & S maintenance depot in Savile Street was closed; and in 1964 the last prewar vehicles were withdrawn, (Nos 336/43 - the ex-B & S rebodied Leyland TD5 and TS7 Longford coaches).

Various single-deck purchases were made during the early 1960s in coach and bus form, including Bedford VAM, VAL and SB chassis with coach bodies from Duple and Plaxton. There were also some AEC Reliances, bringing the coach fleet to some 40 vehicles. A proportion of these were delicensed during the winter months, although there was now a growing tendency to lease or hire bespoke coaches just for the summer period from a local dealer. New buses were Daimler Roadliners, AEC Swifts, and Leyland Leopards and Panthers, with Plaxton, Roe or Marshall bodies. A Leopard in West Riding colours (No. 985) appeared in the demonstration park at the 1962 Earls Court Commercial Motor Show. West Riding was Leyland's biggest independent customer for the Panther, buying 50. Company comments at the time suggested these 1960s acquisitions contained some of the most unreliable vehicles purchased by West Riding since the early1930s. The Daimler Roadliners in particular lasted only seven years, damned by Cummins engine problems. A number of coaches also had short lives with the Company, particularly the Bedford models. This was a reversal of the long service West Riding had obtained from the prewar Leylands and the utility Guys, which appeared to be a sign of the times. Indeed the three last utility Guys finally retired in 1966 after 20 years service. In May 1963 a new bus station opened in Castleford reducing much of the street bus parking in the town.

This was not a happy period for the Company. West Riding faced considerable engineering problems at the time, particularly with the large Wulfrunian fleet, which could not be resolved overnight. A return to more conventional vehicles with a proven record of reliability began in 1966/8 with Leyland Atlantean and Daimler Fleetline double-deckers. Gardner engines removed from

Wulfrunians were used by Daimler to power Fleetlines delivered in 1972.

By 1965 the progressive fleet numbering system had reached over 1000. This was revamped with the new Bedford coach fleet taking fleet numbers 1 upwards and the service fleet commencing at 101 with the new Leyland Atlanteans. However, this system was to be short lived. By 1971 the new company grouping had changed the fleet numbering system again.

1967 - Nationalisation: All Change...

The cost of replacing the Wulfrunian buses was probably a factor in West Riding's decision to sell out to the nationalised Transport Holding Company (shortly to become the National Bus Company) on 30th October 1967, but still operating as an independent subsidiary within the THC. At about the same time the THC purchased another large Yorkshire independent company, Ledgard of Armley, which was absorbed by the West Yorkshire Road Car Company Ltd of Harrogate. The co-owners of County Motors were now all nationalised, consequently there was no need to retain County as a separate operating unit. In 1968, therefore, County Motors was absorbed by Yorkshire Traction. The same year saw the last West Riding red bus disappear, there no longer being a requirement for the historical 'tramway fare' differential.

Under this new management, over 70 Bristol Lodekkas were drafted into the West Riding fleet from sister companies in the NBC, commencing in March 1969, as replacements for the prematurely retired Wulfrunians. Five Dennis Lolines from the Halifax Joint Omnibus Committee were also acquired. Although old fashioned in appearance by this time and generally unpopular with the drivers, who preferred the Wulfrunians, these Bristol Lodekka LD and FLF buses were unequalled in reliability and fulfilled a vital role in reviving the company's fortunes.

It was only a matter of time before the influence of the National Bus Company became apparent, and the first Eastern Coach Works-bodied Bristol RELL single-deckers arrived in 1969. Gradually, the West Riding fleet took on the mantle of the NBC in the

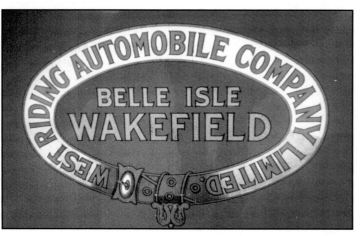

The familiar 'Garter ' motif was to adorn the rear of West Riding buses for over 50 years.

resources. The coaching side of Hebble Motor Services was also taken over and the vehicles transferred to National Travel (North East) Ltd - the coaching arm of NBC; the latter also took over all West Riding tours and express service work. A major market analysis survey brought considerable service changes in late 1981 to the Wakefield and Dewsbury areas, a result of which was the introduction of increased cross-town services.

In late 1982 a combined fleet renumbering scheme put all the group vehicles into type batches. On May 1st 1984 National Travel (East) Ltd also joined the group. This was part of the National Express network set up to bring together all the coaching activities of the constituent operators. The Yorkshire Woollen base at Frost Hill, Liversedge, was used for this purpose, eventually closing in January 1986 when the coaching unit was dispersed to other NBC depots. May 1984 also saw the reconstructed bus station in Pontefract fully reopened.

In 1979 West Riding celebrated its 75th Anniversary. A Bristol VRT and an RELL bus were painted and lined out in the original green and cream colour scheme, as a reminder of their independent past against the corporate image of the day depicted in the NBC livery. The last Lodekkas, which had helped West Riding to reach this anniversary, were withdrawn at this time.

The West Yorkshire Passenger Transport Executive formed an agreement with local National Bus Company subsidiaries in 1981, the aim being to develop a regional integrated transport system. These companies, including West Riding, had already received large subsidies from the local PTE under a national agreement. Consequently, by June 1984 the first West Riding vehicles operating in the PTE area had the 'METRO' fleet name applied and some buses were painted in the PTE's corporate verona green and buttermilk colours. There was some resistance to the move (of having a mix of colours in the fleet) by other

poppy-red livery. In the same year, West Riding's daily express service to Blackpool, inherited from Bullock's, was absorbed by the Yorkshire Pool services. The M1 motorway also reached the West Riding of Yorkshire at this time, opening up new opportunities for fast interurban bus services. West Riding joined a consortium of operators to form the White Rose Expressway linking various towns and cities, which included the major Leeds to Sheffield route. West Riding participated with three Plaxton-bodied Leyland Leopard semi-luxury coaches purchased for this purpose. These were followed by further examples with Plaxton and Alexander coach work. About this time the buses began to lose the familiar 'garter' and tram-type fleet numbers displayed on the rear panels.

In June 1969 a new bus station was opened in Selby, replacing use of the congested Market Place. By 1970 the last of the large fleet of Leyland PD2 Titans was retired.

By 1972 Bristol VRT/ECW double-deckers were entering service. Shortly afterwards the first integral Leyland National single-deckers also joined the fleet, followed eventually by the Phase 2 Nationals in 1982. In 1970 Yorkshire Woollen District (by then another NBC constituent) joined West Riding for administrative purposes but continued to operate as a separate entity within the West Riding Group, as it was known. There was a cross flow of engineering work between the companies as well as the sharing of vehicle

NBC companies operating in the PTE's area; the process of change, therefore, was somewhat slow.

In 1982 the Leyland Olympian double-decker with Eastern Coach Works body became the standard vehicle and large numbers were obtained over the next few years.

In December 1983, history appeared to repeat itself when a joint service with West Yorkshire started between York and South Milford (extended to Pontefract nearly a year later). In 1934 a similar service had been operated by B & S through York to Haxby, and had passed to West Yorkshire as part of a service exchange. However, by 1986 both sections of the service were terminating at Tadcaster. In October 1984 Featherstone depot was closed. This had been the headquarters and first established base of Bullock's over 80 years previously. In 1985 a service between Wakefield and Selby recommenced. It had originally been operated by B & S into the early West Riding era.

1987 - Privatisation again and the final years

The 1985 Transport Act required the National Bus Company, under deregulation conditions, to divest itself of its operating companies to the private sector. Immediately, West Riding took advantage with a number of initiatives. By October 1986 it had formed a subsidiary in Sheffield operating as 'Sheffield and District'. South Yorkshire Transport (of Sheffield) immediately responded by operating in the Wakefield area with 'Compass Buses'. By 1989 both companies had retreated back to their respective bases and the new subsidiaries were eventually absorbed in the areas where they were set up, having exchanged ownership.

During late 1986 the first minibuses arrived in the form of 16-seat Carlyle-bodied Freight Rover Sherpas (Nos M1 - M40 - they were later renumbered in the 400 series), for operation in the Wakefield and Selby districts.

Caldaire Holdings Ltd was the company set up on 30th January 1987 by the local NBC management team, under deregulation conditions, which purchased the West Riding Automobile Company along with Yorkshire Woollen of Dewsbury and the West Yorkshire operations of National Travel (East) Ltd. This also included the Selby and District fleet which was eventually reformed as a separate company. The deal included some 425 vehicles and 1,580 staff. West Riding traded as West Riding Buses and Yorkshire Woollen as Yorkshire Buses. The coastal express services of the former National Express (East) Ltd operated and traded under the Ridings Travel name. West Riding once again operated as an independent company, reverting to its original green and cream fleet livery, with Belle Isle remaining the administration centre for the West Riding Group as it was known. There also continued to be operational movement of vehicles between the individual companies. In 1988 West Riding became one of the first customers to purchase the Leyland National's replacement: the Lynx single-decker. New all-Leyland Royal Tiger coaches arrived fitted out for Ridings Travel and National Express Rapide services. In August 1993, however, the contract with National Express came to an end.

By 1989 the minibus operation required larger vehicles and a batch of Alexander-bodied Dodge S56 25-seat buses was acquired from United Automobile Services (at that time, another Caldaire group company) to replace the Sherpas. By January 1991 the first Optare Metroriders were entering service, replacing the Dodge buses. Over the next five years a total of 57 arrived, and they proved to be very succesful. In 1997 a batch of Mercedes Benz Vario minibuses with Plaxton 25-seat bodies was purchased but these vehicles had a relatively short life. Their disposal signalled a gradual decline in the minibus fleet, being replaced by new low-floor Dennis Darts. Since the demise of the standard Leyland Olympian and Lynx I buses, new orders included Lynx IIs and Volvo B7TLs with Alexander or Plaxton bodies. Dennis Lances, Volvo B10Bs, low-floor DAF buses in single- and double-deck derivatives followed as the company moved through the 1990s into another era.

In 1995 Caldaire Holdings sold out to British Bus Group, leaving West Riding very much to run its own business. By 1996 the Cowie Group had become the owner and eventually rebranded its bus business as Arriva. The West Riding Group of companies became the Yorkshire Bus Group under the new ownership.

In 1994 West Riding acquired one of the oldest established companies in its area, South Yorkshire Road Transport, of Pontefract, along with 18 vehicles which included a number of Leyland Olympians. The history of this company, as that of Bullock's (B & S), with whom it was associated earlier in the last century, is an interesting narrative in itself.

By January 1997 the Savile Street garage in Wakefield had been demolished. It had not been used for a number of years and had been built by Bullock's in the late 1930s.

June 1997 also saw the closure of the Chimes Road 1930s garage at Selby (ex-B & S) and a move to new purpose-built premises in the town at Cowie Way.

On 2nd April 1998 West Riding Automobile Services Ltd became Arriva Yorkshire Ltd; Arriva PLC was the new name for the Cowie Group. Selby and District Transport became Arriva Yorkshire North Ltd; South Yorkshire Road Transport became Arriva Yorkshire South Ltd; and Yorkshire Woollen District became Arriva Yorkshire West Ltd. Later in the year buses began to appear in Arriva's corporate colours. Some 75 years after it first appeared, the distinctive West Riding green and cream livery was being replaced by Arriva's aquamarine and Cotswold stone scheme, with a fleet name of 'Yorkshire'. The last bus painted in the old West Riding colours, a Leyland Lynx registered G332 NUM (332), was withdrawn from service in January 2002, two years before the company would have celebrated the Centenary of the inauguration of its first tramway system in August 1904.

Acknowledgements

I would like to record my appreciation to Michael Bennett and Keith Watson of the West Riding Omnibus Preservation Society (WROPS); Brian Parkin for notes from the Leeds and District Transport News; PSV Circle/Omnibus Society records, and proofreaders David and Mary Shaw for their contribution to this book. Grateful thanks, too, to the various photographers who have so helpfully and willingly made their work available to illustrate this work - where possible photographs are acknowledged individually. Lastly, thanks to John Senior and John Banks of Venture Publications Ltd for their help and enthusiastic support.

David W. Allen FCILT, FILT.
Whitkirk, Leeds
December 2003

Above: Tram **74** is seen in the Bull Ring, Wakefield, just before the system closed in 1932. This tram was originally built for Leeds City Tramways in 1899, and was one of eight purchased from Leeds in 1913. *(David Allen Collection/M J O'Connor)*

Below: Tram **25** at the junction of Wakefield Road and Wood Lane, Rothwell (Bell Hill). *(David Allen Collection/A D Packer)*

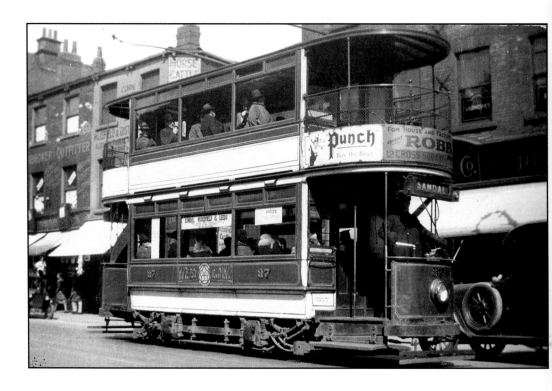

Above: Tram **37** moves along Kirkgate, Wakefield on its way to Sandal. *(David Allen Collection/ M J O'Connor)*

Below: **HL 1376** (**110**), a 1922 Bristol 4-ton model with Bristol 30 seat body, is seen outside Wakefield Cathedral. It was one of the first batch of buses for the fledgling West Riding fleet. It gave seven years' service and when sold was converted to a truck, extending its life a further 15 years. *(David Allen Collection/Bristol Vintage Group)*

Upper: **HL 1801** (**140**) was a 1924 Bristol 4-ton with Bristol 32-seat bodywork. It is shown in delivery condition. After eight years in service it was, like many of the early Bristols, converted for goods use, running well into the 1930s. *(David Allen Collection/ Bristol Vintage Group)*

Centre: **HL 1778** (**153**), a smaller and slightly earlier Bristol, was a 1923 2-ton model with Bristol 20-seat body. The photograph was taken at Belle Isle, Wakefield. After eight years of service, it was scrapped. *(David Allen Collection)*

Lower: **HL 2006** (**163**), a 1924 Bristol 2-ton with Bristol 20-seat body, stands with its proud crew in Bishopgate Street, Leeds, on the Castleford service. Cyril Appleby, on the left, was the driver. The bus was scrapped eight years later. The long gone sign 'Ancient Lights' says it all! *(John Lambert Collection)*

Above: **HL 2927** (**213**), a Leyland PLSC1 Lion with Leyland 31-seat body, was purchased in 1926. This model was the forerunner of the modern half-cab single-decker familiar for the following 30 years. After nine years of West Riding service, it spent some years with Halifax Joint Omnibus Committee. *(John Banks Collection)*

Below: **HL 4545** (**302**), a 1930 Bristol BGW with the manufacturer's 30-seat body, awaiting delivery. The last prewar Bristols were purchased in 1931 and the marque was not bought again until the 1970s. Like many others, this bus spent its last years with a showman, in this case until 1948. *(David Allen Collection/Bristol Vintage Group)*

Above: **HL 4549** (**306**) was another of the 1930 Bristol BGWs, seen on a summer day trip to Scarborough. It was parked on Marine Drive, a useful and convenient parking spot that was later denied to coach operators by the local authority. *(John Banks Collection/G H F Atkins)*

Below: The first Leyland TD1 Titan lowbridge double deckers, part of a batch of four (252-5), delivered in 1928 with Leyland open-staircase bodies seating 51, photographed at Belle Isle, Wakefield. The background provides a poignant reminder of what was about to be replaced. *(John Banks Collection)*

Above: **HL 3821** (**254**), one of the 1928 Leyland TD1 Titans, in an interesting view of the rear end. Within two years the open staircase design would become obsolete.

Below: Leyland TD1 **HL 3819** (**252**) of 1928 - the very first double-decker purchased by West Riding - was photographed making its way out of Wakefield along Doncaster Road, Crofton, in scenery which is identifiable 75 years later. *(Both: John Banks Collection)*

Above: **HL 3820 (253)**, one of the 1928 Leyland TD1s, on a wet day in Aire Street, Castleford, passing the old Star Picture Palace. It had a life of ten years with West Riding.

Below: Number **252** again, attracting attention in Westgate, Wakefield. After ten years with the Company the bus was sold and rebodied as a coach in the London area, where it ran until 1955. *(Both: John Banks Collection)*

Above: **HL 3818** (**251**), a 1928 Leyland PLSC 3 fitted with a 30-seat Davidson body, photographed approaching Oulton Lodge on the journey from Leeds to Doncaster. It was withdrawn in 1936.

Below: The all-Leyland TD1 - the workhorse of many early bus fleets. This West Riding example gives a clear view of the Company's "bow-tie" motif. *(Both: John Banks Collection)*

HL 4467 (270), first of the last (1929) batch of open-staircase Leyland TD1 buses for West Riding, showing the tramway type fleet number together with the "garter" which was to be a feature on buses and coaches for many years to come. This vehicle, one of a batch of eight, operated for West Riding until 1938. *(Both: John Banks Collection)*

Two views of **HL 4859 (324)**, a 1930 all-Leyland LT2 Lion 32-seater. This bus was to remain in service for 15 years and end its days running for a fairground showman by the name of Harry West. Numerous time-served buses of this type found their way into such fairground fleets, undergoing various types of conversion, usually as equipment haulers but sometimes as living vans. Both varieties were frequently to be seen crawling along from one funfair to the next towing one, two or more trailers. "Showman's" on the tax disc indicated membership of the only licensing group of vehicles legally able to tow multiple trailers. Many remained in use well into the 1960s. *(Both: John Banks Collection)*

HL 5323 (18) was a 1932 Leyland TD2 Titan with Charles H Roe 48-seat centre-entrance highbridge bodywork *(see also page 16)*. Fifty of these buses, painted red (as were the trams prior to 1914) as opposed to West Riding green, were obtained to replace the final Wakefield-based tram system in 1932. All but two were Leylands and it was the start of a long association with both Leyland and Charles H Roe of Crossgates, Leeds. This vehicle was withdrawn in 1948. *(Both: Senior Transport Archive)*

Above: Roe-bodied 48-seat centre-entrance Leyland TD2 Titan **HL 5316** (**11**), dating from 1932, stands in the Bull Ring, Wakefield, before Queen Victoria's statue was moved to Thornes Park (it has since been reinstated). Number 11 and similar vehicles were replaced in 1949 by the new AEC Regent III fleet. *(David Allen Collection)*

Below: **HL 5845** (**49**) was one of a pair of 1933 Guy Arabs (a relatively rare model at that date) with Roe 48-seat centre-entrance bodywork to join the original red fleet. Both were withdrawn in 1948. *(Senior Transport Archive)*

Above: **HL 6370** (**379**) was a 1934 Leyland Lion LT5A model carrying a 32-seat Roe body. This was in a batch originally ordered by Hartley Brothers and Rhodes, of Kippax, who were taken over by West Riding in that year. This vehicle was withdrawn in 1948 and converted by West Riding for use as a service truck, a role it fulfilled until 1956. *(Senior Transport Archive)*

Below: This 1935 Leyland TS7c with all-metal 32-seat bodywork also by Leyland Motors is seen when still very new on Marine Drive, Scarborough, having conveyed a private party to the resort. Its exact identity is unknown, but it was one of a batch of 33, all of which were converted for use as ambulances during the Second World War. Some never returned to West Riding service, others were rebodied by Roe after the hostilities. *(John Banks Collection/G H F Atkins)*

Above: Another of the large 1935 batch of 32-seat all-Leyland TS7c Tigers, **HL 7110** (**420**), was photographed in Barnsley. These TS7c models were among the first of many West Riding "Gearless" Leylands: fitted with a torque converter transmission (signified by the "c" in "TS7c") that was effectively an automatic gearbox. Years before such things were commonplace this system was a great boon to drivers, although not all operators were entirely happy with them and many such vehicles were converted to manual-gearbox specification. This vehicle was another to be used as a wartime ambulance.

Below: The same bus is seen in Cheapside, Barnsley, on the long route between Leeds and Sheffield. HL 7110 was sold by West Riding in 1949 and finished its days as a mobile fish and chip shop in the late 1950s. *(Both: John Banks Collection/G H F Atkins)*

Above: West Riding built up a large fleet of 48-seat Roe-bodied Leyland Titans in the period 1936 to 1942 based on the TD4c, TD5c and TD7 models. The new-profile lowbridge body was regarded as one of the most appealing of bus designs of the day. One of the earlier examples was **HL 7436 (434)** of 1936. The vehicle was reconditioned in 1948 and withdrawn in 1956.

Below: The equivalent standard single-decker in the second half of the 1930s, typified by 1936's TS7c **HL 7535 (461)**, was the Roe-bodied 32-seat Leyland Tiger, of which large numbers were purchased. About this time the distinctive "bow-tie" motif was replaced. The coachbuilders photographed many of their productions at this spot, which is believed to be at the junction of Leeds Ring Road and Coal Road, Seacroft - at that time a very rural area. Number 461 was withdrawn in 1957. *(Both: Senior Transport Archive)*

Above: West Riding had a requirement in 1936 for two 24-seat buses and the Leyland Cub KPZ2 chassis was chosen. Bodywork, as might have been expected, was by Roe. The second of the pair, **HL 7538 (464)**, is illustrated when brand new. A third Cub was acquired in 1939 and all three were withdrawn in 1949. Number 464 then worked for the independent Pritchard, of Newborough, until 1967, when it was acquired for preservation.

Below: One of two semi-luxury buses (although referred to as coaches) delivered in 1936, **HL 7539 (465)** was a Leyland TS7c with a reduced seating capacity of 28 in its Roe bodywork. Withdrawn in 1949, it passed for further service to the Bishop Auckland independent OK Motor Services, who used it until 1960. *(Both: Senior Transport Archive)*

Above: This was one of an additional five buses (51-5) delivered in 1936 for the red fleet. They had Leyland TD4c chassis fitted with the new-profile Roe body, which gave a clear view of the central entrance and staircase system. They, or rather the drivers, also had the luxury of the "Gearless" transmission, a supreme advantage on the multi-stop former tram routes. *(Senior Transport Archive)*

Below: **HL 7682 (54)** of the same batch is seen on the Leeds stand in the old Bull Ring in Wakefield. After twelve years of West Riding service the vehicle was sold. It was rebodied as a coach and operated by Victoria Coaches, of Leigh-on-Sea, until 1955. *(David Allen Collection)*

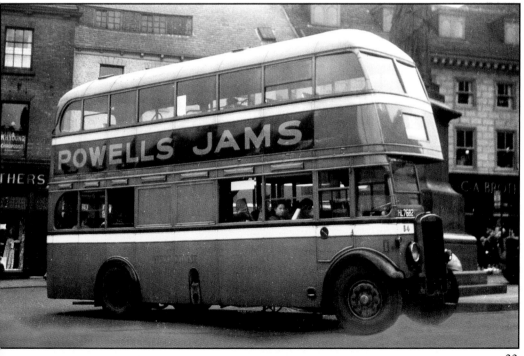

Above: **HL 6633** (**407**) was a Leyland TS7c with Roe bodywork. New in July 1935, it was originally fitted with a Leyland body. Used as a wartime ambulance, it was returned to West Riding and rebodied by Roe in 1949. The vehicle was withdrawn from passenger service as a 28-year-old in 1963; its final days thence until November 1966 were spent at Selby as the depot tow bus. It thus served the Company for a total of 31½ years. *(David Allen Collection)*

Below: **HL 7515** (**441**) and **HL 9073** (**544**), respectively Leyland TS7c and TS8c Tigers with Roe 32-seat bodywork, photographed at the Springs terminus in Wakefield before the new bus station was opened in 1952. By 1957 both vehicles had been withdrawn and scrapped. The adjoining bus stop shows departure points for Walton, New Crofton, Newstead and Brierley - all original mining villages south of Wakefield. *(Alan Cross)*

Above: A Chimes Road, Selby scene features **HL 8220** (**487**), a 1937 Leyland TS7 with the familiar Roe bodywork. It was the first West Riding bus sent to this former Bullock depot shortly after the takeover of that operator. HL 8220 was scrapped in 1957. *(David Allen Collection/R F Mack)*

Below: An action shot of the driver entering the cab of 1937 Leyland TS7 Tiger **HL 8221** (**488**) in the Springs, Wakefield. Rear views of the older vehicle types are rare. This was another West Riding vehicle scrapped in 1957. *(Alan Cross)*

Above: Leyland TD4c/Roe **HL 6072** (**505**), dating from 1937, was loaned to Sheffield and London in 1940/1. Here it is outside London Bridge Station. It was withdrawn in 1949 and joined the fleet of Barton Transport Ltd, Chilwell. *(David Allen Collection/W J Haynes)*

Below: **HL 7116** (**426**), a 1935 Leyland TS7c/Roe, is seen working as an ambulance at Seacroft Hospital, Leeds, sometime after the war. It is doubtful whether it returned to passenger service before disposal in 1949, upon which it passed through the hands of various dealers and Welsh independent operators, surviving thus until September 1953. *(WROPS)*

Above: West Riding managed to secure a large fleet of austerity (or utility) Guy Arabs once they became available in the later stages of the Second World War. **AHL 45 (588)**, a 1944 Arab II model bodied by Roe, is pictured in the Springs, Wakefield. The wartime Guys gave long service in all parts of West Riding's operating area and, as happened elsewhere, led to the operator buying Guy chassis in the postwar period. Number 588 was withdrawn in 1965. *(Alan Cross)*

Below: **HL 9992 (574)** was a 1943 Guy Arab I, again with the ubiquitous Roe bodywork. It is seen in the Market Place, Selby. Selby depot was to receive many of these Guys in their later years and the frequent service to York was supported by the Guy fleet. Number 574 was withdrawn in 1963. *(David Allen Collection/R F Mack)*

Above: **AHL 101** (**599**), a 1945 Guy Arab II/Roe, in Wakefield bus station. This bus had a long service life (it was one of the last withdrawals of the type in 1966), most of which was spent at Belle Isle alongside many of the other utilities. *(Geoff Coxon)*

Below: **HL 9955** (**570**), another utility Guy Arab I/Roe, this one dating from 1942, was photographed in the rural area between York and Doncaster on a Selby-based service. Withdrawn in 1962, this had been the first utility Guy in the West Riding fleet, and the only one to arrive before 1943. When new it was fitted with a Gardner 5LW engine, eventually replaced with a 6LW to conform to the specification of the 1943-6 Guy Arabs. *(David Allen Collection)*

Above: **AHL 110 (608)**, a 1945 Guy Arab II, is seen, as refurbished in 1948, in Leeds Central bus station. It was one of the later deliveries of utility buses and its Roe body was to the 'relaxed utility' style that preceded the resumption of normal peacetime production. The bus was in service until 1965. *(David Allen Collection/R F Mack)*

Below: 1943 utility Guy Arab II **HL 9957 (572)** at the Piccadilly terminus in York. The Roe body shown came from a 1939 TD7 in 1950. HL 9957 was withdrawn in 1963. *(David Allen Collection)*

Above: **AHL 656** (**61**), an RT-type 1946 AEC Regent III with Roe centre-entrance bodywork. This was one of a small batch of provincial RTs, with London-type low-profile radiators, which were the first replacements for the original red fleet. It is seen here in the small Cross York Street bus station in Leeds. *(David Allen Collection/R F Mack)*

Below: Roe-bodied **BHL 331** (**75**) was a 1948 example of the more common version of the AEC Regent lll, with higher radiator profile, found outside London. It was at the former Corn Exchange tram terminus in Leeds, which was in use until 1956. By 1961 this bus had been withdrawn. Service 10, the direct route to Wakefield, eventually became 110 as operated by Arriva at the time of writing. *(David Allen Collection/R F Mack)*

Above: Another of the 1948 AEC Regent III/Roe vehicles, **BHL 590 (92)**, moving out of Park Street, Selby, on a local service. A number of the centre-entrance red-fleet buses were painted green and transferred to other duties, mostly in Castleford or Selby as in this case. There were objections from some of the travelling public when this type of bus was operated in purely rural areas because of safety hazards connected with the central staircase. *(David Allen Collection/R F Mack)*

Below: The equivalent AEC single-decker at this time was the Regal III. **BHL 694 (652)** was a 1948 example, one of a small number bought about this time. It lasted in service for 18 years. *(John Banks Collection/G H F Atkins)*

Above: **BHL 800** (**653**), a 1948 Leyland PD2 with bodywork by Leyland, at Chimes Road depot, Selby. This was one of a small number of highbridge Leylands in the green fleet. Six were sent to Selby soon after the Bullock takeover - 653 being one. In their later years, all 16 vehicles in the highbridge fleet were operated from Selby. *(Glen Trickett Collection)*

Below: **BHL 863** (**662**), a 1949 Leyland-bodied highbridge 56-seat Leyland Titan PD2/1, stands in Selby Market Place, working on the long service between Leeds and Goole. Utility Guys can also be seen in this late 1950s scene. *(David Allen Collection/Omnibus Society)*

BHL 899 (**111**), a 1949 AEC Regent III with Roe 50-seat centre-entrance bodywork, seen at Belle Isle. This red-fleet bus was bought for preservation but has not survived. *(Geoff Coxon)*

<< *Opposite page:* **BHL 891** (**103**), another of the 1949 AEC Regent IIIs, seen at the Corn Exchange terminus for the red fleet in Leeds. This arrangement was superseded in December 1956 when a dedicated bus station was opened in Cross York Street. *(John Banks Collection/G H F Atkins)*

Above: **CHL 160** (**689**), a 1950 all-Leyland PD2/1 in Wakefield bus station. It gave 19 years of service, in contrast to the 1963 Wulfrunian **VHL 957** (**957**), which lasted only six. *(Malcolm King)*

Below: **BHL 864** (**663**), a 1949 all-Leyland highbridge PD2/1, is illustrated in Piccadilly, York, adjacent to the original Airspeed factory - which had long since changed hands - about to commence one of the longest of West Riding's services: to Selby and Doncaster. *(David Allen Collection)*

Above: **DHL 922** (**711**), one of ten 1952 Roe-bodied lowbridge 50-seat AEC Regent IIIs, in Leeds Central bus station after the latter's 1963 rebuilding. The bus was withdrawn in 1966. *(Geoff Coxon)*

Below: Another of the batch, **DHL 927** (**716**), also in Leeds. Behind is a South Yorkshire Motors Leyland PD2. *(John Banks Collection/G H F Atkins)*

>> *Opposite page:* **EHL 334** (**723**), a 1952 Leyland PS2/13A fitted with Roe 35-seat coachwork to the then newly permissible 30ft length. This vehicle was based at Belle Isle for most of its life. It was one of six: the first purpose-built coaches purchased by West Riding; all six were withdrawn in1965. *(John Banks Collection/G H F Atkins)*

<< Opposite page: Another of the recently introduced 30-footers of the early fifties, **EHL 337 (726)** was a 1952 Leyland PS2/12A service bus with Roe 39-seat bodywork. In a rarely photographed scene, it is on the Selby toll bridge. This bus was allocated new to Selby depot, shortly after the Bullock takeover, and was transferred to Castleford in 1961. It was withdrawn in 1969. *(David Allen Collection)*

This page: Four of the six all-Leyland lowbridge PD2/12 Titans delivered in 1953 carried a patriotic red, white and blue livery to commemorate the Coronation of Queen Elizabeth II. The buses so treated were Nos 739-42 (EHL 831-4); Nos 743/4 (EHL 835/6) were delivered in West Riding red livery, to be repainted green in 1954. *(Geoff Coxon; John Banks Collection)*

Above: **EHL 834** (**742**), one of the 1953 all-Leyland PD2/12s that had carried the Coronation livery when new, photographed in Wakefield bus station in normal livery. It was withdrawn in 1970. *(John Banks Collection/G H F Atkins)*

Below: **EHL 836** (**744**), another of the 1953 all-Leyland PD2/12s. It was one of the two which ran for a short time in red livery on the red routes before being repainted green. Being somewhat distinctive they were referred to as "trackies" - after the similar local Yorkshire Traction livery. *(John Banks Collection)*

>> *Opposite page:* Six more all-Leyland lowbridge PD2/12s, Nos 745-50, were delivered in 1953, and these had standard green livery from the outset. **FHL 111** (**745**) represents the batch, which had some of the last classic "Farington" style bodies before Leyland ceased body production. Records indicate that this particular bus when new was a "Show exhibit", but it is not known whether this referred to a Commercial Motor Show. *(John Banks Collection)*

51

Above: **FHL 987** (**751**) was a 1954 Seddon Pennine, bodied as a 44-seat, front-entrance service bus by Duple. It was photographed in Leeds Central bus station on its regular duty - service 169 to Castleford and Fryston. It was one of a small number of buses obtained from Seddon in this period. It was later transferred to Selby for use on the rural services in that area and was withdrawn in 1963.

Below: With the demise of Leyland-produced bodywork Roe once again became the favoured supplier, in 1954 building a batch of ten lowbridge 50-seaters on Leyland PD2/22 Titan chassis. The enclosed radiator, widely known as "tin-front styling", was becoming popular at this time, and this batch of buses featured a version of it developed for Midland Red. **GHL 309** (**760**) was in Marshgate bus station, Doncaster, awaiting departure on service 152 to Leeds via Pontefract and Castleford. (*Both: John Banks Collection/G H F Atkins*)

Above: Many operators were so impressed by the ruggedness and reliability of the wartime Guy Arab chassis that they carried on buying them from 1946 onwards; West Riding waited a decade before returning to the Wolverhampton chassis maker and in 1955 took delivery of 20 Guy Arab IV chassis fitted with lowbridge 53-seat bodywork by Roe. A further 50 similar chassis were brought into service over the next two years. **GHL 715 (766)** was in Sheffield on the long service to Leeds.

Below: AEC Reliance underfloor-engined coaches and service buses began to appear in 1956. **JHL 712 (812)**, one of twelve Roe-bodied 44-seater buses, was photographed in Marshgate bus station Doncaster on local service 133 to Askern. It and No. 813 worked from new out of Selby depot. Withdrawn in 1969, it gave further service in the North-East in the fleet of Martindale's Coaches, Ferryhill. *(Both: John Banks Collection/G H F Atkins)*

<< *Opposite page:* **AHL 693 (787)**, a rebuilt 1947 Leyland PS1/Roe double-decker, features in this delightful period scene in Selby. It was one of a number of former Bullock single-deckers rebodied in 1956 after chassis rebuilds at Belle Isle. The scheme overcame an immediate shortage of double-deck capacity at the time and gave the buses a further service life of some 10 years. *(David Allen Collection/R F Mack)*

Above: **AHL 806 (790)**, another of the rebuilt 1947 Leyland PS1/Roe vehicles, in Piccadilly, York. Being somewhat under powered, many of these rebodied single-deckers operated over the flat Vale of York from Selby depot. *(David Allen Collection/R F Mack)*

Below: **JHL 985 (805)**, a 1957 AEC Reliance with Roe Dalesman 41-seat coachwork, one of a number of this type, lasted until 1966. Belle Isle, Savile Street and Castleford depots had allocations of this type. *(Keith Watson Collection)*

Above: **SHL 918** (918) was a 1961 AEC Reliance fitted with Plaxton 41-seat centre-entrance coachwork. It was on private hire work, possibly in the Lake District. This coach was one of six used on the Wakefield to Blackpool express service amongst other duties. They were withdrawn in 1965/6 and all found further service with other operators. *(Keith Watson Collection)*

Below: **THL 928** (928) was another 1961 AEC Reliance, this time carrying Roe dual-doorway bodywork for one-man operation: one of twelve that entered service that year from Belle Isle and Selby depots. Withdrawn in 1973, it was shipped to Jamaica with similar buses for further use. *(WROPS)*

>> *Opposite page upper:* **OHL 863** (863) was the 1959 Guy Wulfrunian/Roe 75-seat prototype of this revolutionary but not very successful bus. West Riding was heavily involved in and committed to the Wulfrunian project and was to receive most of the production over the next five years. Number 863 appeared at the Scottish Commercial Motor Show in that year. Because of the vehicle's programme of demonstration duties for Guy Motors West Riding did not have full use of it until

1961. It was withdrawn in 1969, giving longer service than many of the other West Riding Wulfrunians. *(David Allen Collection)*

Below: **OHL 863** (**863**) was operated on the red bus routes as originally intended, but as production increased and the ex-tram routes no longer required any differential treatment, the red fleet became green, including 863, in 1966. It is seen here in Borough Road adjacent to the old bus station. Today the same location is Platform 1 of the "new" bus station. *(Glen Trickett Collection)*

Above: The production Wulfrunian 75-seaters were sadly short-lived: **THL 880 (880)**, for example, was in service for only seven years. Delivered in red and cream in 1961, it was in a batch of 20 used to convert service 10 (Leeds - Wakefield - Kettlethorpe) to full Wulfrunian operation. The picture was taken in Leeds Central bus station and the bus was on a service to Castleford and Wakefield. *(Geoff Coxon)*

Below: Roe-bodied Wulfrunian **THL 897 (897)** of 1961 approaches Wakefield along Horbury Road at its junction with Broadway on service 20 from Ossett, one of the ex-tram routes. This service was converted to Wulfrunian operation with the first deliveries in January 1961. Number 897 was withdrawn in 1970. *(John Banks)*

Above: **BHL 356C** (**1005**), a 1965 Guy Wulfrunian/Roe, is seen in Leeds Central bus station in November 1968 - half way through its short life. It had entered service in full green and cream livery as one of the last batch of 30 to be delivered in 1965.

Below: An earlier Wulfrunian, **THL 890** (**890**) of 1961, leaves Leeds Central bus station in the same period. The vehicle has the darker Tilling green livery with single cream band introduced in February 1968. It survived for 11 years. *(Both: T W Moore)*

Above: **WHL 990** (**990**) was a 1963 Leyland PSU3/1R Leopard with Plaxton 53-seat bodywork, one of seven delivered in 1962/3. It was in Leeds Central bus station operating its regular service 82 to Hemsworth. Most of this type were based at Castleford depot. Number 990 survived until 1977. Number 985 of the batch was exhibited at the 1962 Commercial Motor Show. *(Geoff Coxon)*

Below: **BHL 524C** (**1038**), a 1965 Bedford SB5 with Duple Northern Firefly 41-seat coachwork. One of a batch of six, there were also six similar chassis bodied by Plaxton. These twelve brought the total coach fleet to forty. Ten of the Bedfords, including this one, were quickly withdrawn (in 1967) and the other two in 1971. *(John Lambert Collection)*

Above: **EHL 471D** (**2**), one of three 1966 Bedford VAL/Plaxton 52-seat coaches. This was in a new fleet numbering series which was to change again in 1971, the year in which the coach was withdrawn. *(John Lambert Collection)*

Below: The policy of purchasing lightweight coaches in 1966 included nine Bedford VAM5 models equipped with Plaxton 45-seat coachwork, and there would be a further six in 1967. The first of them, **EHL 461D** (**4**) stands at Selby depot in the late 1960s. All 15 were withdrawn in 1971. *(Keith Watson)*

Above: After the Wulfrunian experience West Riding turned to rear-engined double-deckers, beginning in 1966 with a batch of 25 Roe-bodied 76-seat Leyland PDR1/2 Atlanteans, originally allocated to Belle Isle and represented by **FHL 766D** (**117**). The last of the batch, No. 125, was exhibited at the 1966 Commercial Motor Show. Number 117 was withdrawn in 1980. *(David Allen Collection)*

Below: **FHL 827D** (**134**) was a 1966 Daimler Roadliner SRC6 with Plaxton 50-seat service-bus bodywork, one of ten purchased that year - the first of these models produced by Daimler. Engine problems gave them a short life and No. 134, seen here leaving Leeds Central bus station, was sold in1973, although it operated elsewhere for a few more years. *(Geoff Coxon)*

Above: The mid-sixties cannot have been a happy time for West Riding's engineers. Following what with hindsight can only be described as the disastrous Wulfrunian (and by 1967 this would have been more than evident), the Daimler Roadliner brought its own peculiar brand of difficulties, and then the AEC Swift - not AEC's most successful model - was tried. **JHL 819E** (**19**) was the first of five 1967 Swifts fitted out by Marshall, of Cambridge, as 47-seat dual-purpose vehicles. It is seen on the Goole - Selby - Leeds service. All five were allocated to Selby depot, on whose longer routes the dual-purpose seating was an advantage. All were withdrawn in 1976.

Below: Nor was the Panther much of a feather in Leyland's cap. West Riding bought a batch of 45, also in 1967, bodied by Marshall or Roe as 51-seat service buses. One of the Marshall examples, **KHL 647F** (**147**), in NBC livery, was parked in Pontefract. It gave 11 years of service. *(Both: Geoff Coxon)*

Above: **MHL 299F** (**634**), a 1968 Roe-bodied 76-seat Daimler Fleetline, leaving Pontefract bus station. After the large number of Leyland Atlanteans purchased in 1967, West Riding placed orders with Daimler for its 1968/9 intake of double-deckers, retaining Roe for bodies. Periscopes were eventually fitted to most of these buses, as well as to the Atlanteans, for one-man operation.

Below: **NHL 532F** (**32**), one of a trio of 1968 Leyland Leopard/Plaxton 49-seater dual-purpose buses mainly used on the then new local interurban M1 motorway express services. By the time of this photograph it had been repainted in the NBC's white and poppy-red "local coach" livery. *(Both: Geoff Coxon)*

Above: **XNU 424** (**401**), a 1955 Bristol LD6G Lodekka ex-Midland General, was one of the first of the large fleet of Lodekkas drafted in from sister NBC companies in 1969 to replace the Wulfrunians. It is seen in the Royston area, and was withdrawn in 1971. *(John Lambert Collection)*

Below: Another of the Wulfrunian replacements was **EHT 106C** (**441**), a 1965 Bristol FLF Lodekka from the Bristol Omnibus Company. Joining the West Riding fleet in 1969, it remained in service until 1980, thence passing to the Lincolnshire Road Car Company. It was photographed entering Leeds Central bus station. *(Geoff Coxon)*

Above: Here is another of the 1967 Leyland Panthers, this time the Roe-bodied version. **JHL 144E** (**144**) stands in Wheldon Road depot, Castleford. It gave 11 years of service. West Riding was one of Leyland's largest customers for this model. *(Keith Watson)*

Below: **THL 257H** (**257**), a 1970 Bristol RELL6G with Eastern Coach Works 53-seat bodywork, photographed in Leeds City bus station. It had an 11 year life with West Riding. A small fleet of this model was built up over the next three years. *(Geoff Coxon)*

Above: **FCP 300E** (**464**), a 1967 Dennis Loline III bodied by Northern Counties, enters Leeds Central bus station. This was one of five similar buses obtained from the Halifax Joint Omnibus Committee in the same period as the Lodekkas. Although of a similar design, they had a higher seating capacity, at 74 against 70, than the FLF Lodekka, and gave a further eight years of service.

Below: **GHD 414G** (**267**), a 1969 Alexander-bodied 53-seat Leyland Leopard, seen well out of home territory in Worswick Street, Newcastle. This vehicle had been new to Yorkshire Woollen in 1969 before passing to Hebble and then to West Riding in 1971 along with four more coaches from the same batch. All five were withdrawn in 1980. *(Both: Geoff Coxon)*

Above: **WHL 276J** (**674**), one of twelve 1971 Alexander-bodied Daimler Fleetline 76-seaters, seen on a local servce in Pontefract bus station. These were among the first of a substantial number of Alexander-bodied double-deckers obtained over the next few years.

Below: A 1972 batch of 25 Daimler CRG6LX Fleetlines had 76-seat bodies built by the Northern Counties Motor and Engineering Company Ltd, of Wigan, epitomised by **BHL 611K** (**711**) in Leeds Central bus station with the once familiar backdrop of Quarry Hill flats.This was one of the Fleetlines powered by engines from withdrawn Wulfrunians. *(Both: Geoff Coxon)*

Above: **HWY 724N** (**384**), a 1975 Leyland Leopard/Alexander 49-seat coach, was one of the second batch of coaches brought in for the White Rose interurban express services, operated jointly with other operators after the extension of the M1 motorway into West Yorkshire. A Leyland Leopard/Plaxton dual-purpose bus stands alongside.

Below: West Riding became part of THC empire in 1967 and thus passed into National Bus Company control on 1st January 1969. Following the loan of RELL6G demonstrator LAE 770E in 1968, the first new Bristol single-deck chassis arrived in 1969 and, as we have seen, membership of the NBC permitted the rapid influx of Lodekkas to replace the ailing Wulfrunian fleet. The first new Bristol VRs came in 1973 and the type was a regular arrival through the rest of the 1970s. **OWW 904P** (**760**), a 1976 example with ECW bodywork, is seen in the familiar surroundings of Leeds Central bus station. *(Both: Geoff Coxon)*

Above: Duple-bodied Leyland Leopard **RYG 397R** (**6**), dating from 1977, is shown in the transfer livery of the joint (with Yorkshire Woollen) coach fleet in Leeds Central bus station. It was working the joint X32 Leeds to Sheffield express service.

Below: **CWX 656T** (**38**), a 1978 Leyland National I, was in a batch of 15 purchased in that year to augment the growing National fleet. *(Both: Geoff Coxon)*

Above: **EWX 214Y** (**214**), a 1982 Leyland National 2 in the subsidiary Selby and District fleet, leaving Doncaster Northern bus station for a short working to Askern. Like other vehicles thus allocated at that time, it carried the fleet name West Riding Selby.

Below: **C615 ANW** (**615**), a 1985 Leyland Olympian/ECW, operating the Sheffield - Leeds express service. Large numbers of this model were purchased from 1982 including No. 615, one of six in coach configuration for interurban express services, branded in the later 1980s as Fastaway. *(Both: Geoff Coxon)*

Above: **B597 SWX** (**597**), a 1984 Leyland Olympian/ECW leaving Doncaster Northern bus station in the Verona green of the short-lived West Yorkshire PTE Metro livery.

Below: An ECW-bodied Leyland Olympian in NBC poppy-red livery: **EWX 535Y** (**535**), a 1983 entry into the fleet, was photographed at the beginning of a journey to Selby and York from Doncaster, operated by Selby and District. *(Both: Geoff Coxon)*

Above: **WWA 300Y** (**55**), a 1983 Leyland Tiger with Plaxton coachwork, originated with National Travel (East) Ltd and came into the coaching arm of the West Riding Group when National Travel was disbanded in 1986. *(Geoff Coxon)*

Below: **EWX 213Y** (**213**), a 1983 Leyland National 2, causes a traffic problem in Park Street as it turns towards Selby bus station, its main operating base. At this time in the late 1980s, buses were receiving the Caldaire-style livery of green and cream as shown. *(Keith Watson)*

Above: **CWR 518Y** (**518**), a 1982 Eastern Coach Works-bodied Leyland Olympian, one of a number operating with Selby and District from West Riding's large fleet, was photographed in Selby working on the long route from York to Doncaster.

Below: **D830 KWT** (**430**) was a 1987 Freight Rover Sherpa bodied by Carlyle. It was photographed on a Wakefield local service in Lupset. Nearly 40 of these 16-seat minibuses appeared in the fleet at this time as the Company came to terms with rising costs and falling traffic. Most operated from the Belle Isle and Selby depots. *(Both: Keith Watson)*

Above: A variation on the minibus theme: **E508 HHN** (**454**) was an Alexander-bodied 1987 Dodge S56 25-seater. It was photographed in Park Street, Selby. A call for larger minibuses brought No. 454 and 21 stablemates from sister Caldaire company, United Automobile Services, of Darlington, in the late 1980s. They worked for West Riding for about five years. *(Keith Watson)*

Below: **JYG 423V** (**768**), a 1979 Eastern Coach Works-bodied Leyland Atlantean, was one of twelve West Riding Atlanteans, originating from the Yorkshire Woollen District fleet, that were drafted into the short-lived Sheffield and District subsidiary. It is shown on a local service leaving Sheffield bus station. *(Geoff Coxon)*

Above: **E262 TUB (262)**, a 1988 Leyland Lynx, is seen on a local service in Sheffield as part of West Riding's early expansion plans after deregulation.

Below: **JHL 856L (110)**, a 1973 Leyland National I transferred from the main fleet (where it had been fleet number 356), had a short life in the subsidiary Sheffield and District fleet. It is seen in the original Caldaire-style livery but it soon received the standard blue and white of Sheffield and District. The picture illustrates it operating a Sheffield local service. *(Both: Geoff Coxon)*

Above: **C36 CWT** (**36**), a 1986 Leyland Tiger/Plaxton 49-seat coach, one of ten brought into service during that year, is seen at Wheldon Road depot, Castleford. Their duties included interurban express services and National Express work. The latter ceased in 1993.

Below: Duple-bodied Leyland Leopard coach **DAK 218V** (**218**), which dated from 1979, was transferred from National Travel (East) Ltd into the Sheffield & District fleet. It is seen after being repainted in the red and white Fastaway livery for the urban express services introduced in October 1986. It was allocated to Castleford depot for its new role. *(Both: Keith Watson)*

Above: **C220 CWW (220)**, an impressive Auwaerter Neoplan/Plaxton 71-seat coach, is shown leaving Wellington Street bus station, Leeds, on the last leg of its National Express journey from London in June 1986. As part of the West Riding Group, National Travel (East) provided 220 as one of a pair for service 561 (Bradford - Leeds - London) before the vehicles were given West Riding fleet names and numbers. *(Keith Watson)*

Below: AEC Matador recovery truck **A2**, running on trade plates **158 HL**. A fleet story cannot be complete without reference to the vehicles rarely seen in public (one hopes). The Castleford based ex-military truck is pictured in Leeds Central bus station. *(Glen Trickett Collection)*

Above: Belle Isle depot, Wakefield, originally built for the tram fleet, showing the old welding and paint shop. **KHL 848 (848)**, a 1957 Guy Arab IV/Roe stands outside.

Below: Wheldon Road depot, Castleford, was also constructed for the separate tram system. It is shown here much refurbished for a modern bus fleet. Rear-engined double- and single-deckers are visible, as well as a half-cab Guy Arab. *(Both: John Churms Collection)*

Above: Wakefield bus station opened in 1952 with some ceremony. It survived nearly 50 years before being replaced and redeveloped in 2001. The single-decker is **PHL 237G** (**237**), a 1969 Plaxton-bodied Leyland Panther.

Below: A variety of buses in the original Wakefield bus station are seen with a backdrop of Savile Street bus depot (ex-Bullock). *(Both: John Churms Collection)*

Wakefield & District Light Railways Company.

YORKSHIRE (WEST RIDING) ELECTRIC TRAMWAYS COMPANY, LIMITED,

Central Office,

H. ENGLAND,
General Manager

D'd by
A/5

Belle Isle,

Wakefield, Tues. 27th Feb. 1923

In your reply please quote

ALL COMMUNICATIONS TO BE ADDRESSED TO THE GENERAL MANAGER.

West Riding in Colour

Above: An overprinted letterheading from 1923. The stocks of paper dated from at least 14 years earlier. *(Senior Transport Archive)*

Below: **OWW 906P** (**762**), a 1976 Bristol VRT/ECW, stands in Leeds Central bus station, displaying the traditional green West Riding livery applied for the Company's 75th anniversary in 1979. The bus contrasted sharply with the ubiquitous and mundane NBC poppy-red livery of the day. *(Geoff Coxon)*

Above: **AHL 47** (**590**), a 1945 Guy Arab II/Roe, was one of the large wartime utility fleet. It gave 19 years of service. It is seen pulling away from Sovereign Street terminus in Leeds. Behind is **HHL 996** (**784**), a Guy Arab IV/ Roe, one of a batch of five built with ultra low bodies for negotiating the low bridge at Fitzwilliam on service 82/83 Leeds - Hemsworth. *(Malcolm King)*

Below: **BHL 883** (**95**), a 1949 AEC Regent III of the red fleet, in the classic setting of the Corn Exchange terminus, Leeds, which the buses shared with Leeds trams until moving to the bespoke station in Cross York Street in late 1956. *(David Allen Collection/Leeds Transport Historical Society)*

Above: **BHL 899 (111)**, a 1949 AEC Regent III with Roe bodywork, of the type so long familiar in and characteristic of the West Riding fleet, was one of the last batch of red-fleet centre-entrance buses. It was withdrawn in 1964 and was the subject of a failed attempt at preservation. *(David Allen Collection)*

Below: **BHL 902 (114)**, another of the 1949 Roe-bodied centre-entrance AEC Regent IIIs, was one of the few red-fleet AECs to join the green fleet in later years. Number 114 is seen in Lower Westgate, Wakefield, on a local service - the 114 to Flanshaw Estate. *(John Banks Collection)*

Above: Nineteen-forty-eight AEC Regal III **BHL 693** (**651**) is seen at Wheldon Road depot, Castleford. One of a batch of six Roe-bodied front-entrance 32-seaters obtained in that year, it gave 18 years' service.

Below: **BHL 865** (**664**), a 1949 all-Leyland PD2 56-seater, one of only 16 highbridge buses in the green fleet, was waiting for the photographer in Marshgate bus station, Doncaster. Like most of the type, it was based at Selby for the longer routes operated from that depot. *(Both: David Allen Collection)*

Above: **EHL 832** (**740**), one of the four 1953 all-Leyland PD2/12 Titans painted in a temporary special livery for the Coronation, heels over as it turns in Selby market place. The bus was based at Selby and gave free rides over the short celebratory period. *(David Allen Collection)*

Below: **KHL 854** (**854**), a 1957 Guy Arab IV/Roe, photographed in Leeds Central bus station. West Riding's Guy fleet, already substantial, continued to grow at this time as West Riding moved away from Leyland, its traditional supplier. Number 854 was one of a large batch of 45 buses, which were noteworthy in having rear platform doors fitted to improve passenger comfort, particularly on the longer journeys in winter. All five depots received examples as they were delivered. *(Malcolm King)*

Above: Roe-bodied 1947 Leyland Tiger PS1 **AHL 810 (793)** was originally a Bullock single-decker. It was rebodied in 1956 as seen, extending its life to 1967. It is seen here at Halton Dial, Leeds, on the long service from Goole.

Below: AEC Reliance/Roe 44-seat service bus **JHL 714 (814)** of 1956 is seen in Wakefield bus station. The Company's commitment to the high capacity single-decker brought in vehicles whose seating capacity was only four fewer than that of their prewar Leyland Titan double-deckers. *(Both: David Allen Collection)*

Above: The well-documented **OHL 863** (**863**), the 1959 Guy Wulfrunian/Roe, which was the first to be operated by West Riding, makes its way out of Leeds along Hunslet Road on the Rothwell (former tram) service. *(David Allen Collection)*

Below: The West Riding livery contrast: **THL 880** (**880**), one of the 1961 Guy Wulfrunians, fortuitously caught parked alongside similar vehicle **VHL 940** (**940**) of the following year. By 1969 both had been withdrawn. *(Malcolm King)*

Above: Castleford depot was the allocation point for 1963 Plaxton-bodied 53-seat Leyland PSU3/1R Leopard **WHL 990** (**990**), seen here in Leeds Central bus station. It was one of the first buses built to the then new maximum length of 36 feet to join the West Riding fleet. *(Malcolm King)*

Below: **EHL 472D** (**3**), a 1966 Bedford VAL14 with Plaxton coachwork, had six years' service with West Riding, and after sale ran with various operators until 1980. The vehicle alongside, **JHL 983** (**803**) of 1957, was an AEC Reliance with stylish Roe Dalesman coachwork. It was from one of the more successful batches of West Riding coaches, which gave much longer service. This vehicle passed into preservation in 1978. *(Malcolm King Collection/J C Leadbetter)*

Above: **HHL 716E** (**16**), one of the 1967 Bedford VAM chassis with Plaxton 45-seat coachwork, is seen at Coliseum coach park in Blackpool. Number 16 was one of the batch of six that provided team coaches for Wakefield Trinity and Featherstone Rovers rugby league clubs. The whole batch was withdrawn and sold in1971, all finding new owners. *(Malcolm King Collection/J C Leadbetter)*

Below: **LHL 164F** (**164**), a 1967 Leyland Panther with 51-seat bodywork by Roe. Others of this large batch of Panthers had bodies by Marshall. LHL 164F eventually went into preservation after a spell of driver-training service as fleet No. A26. *(David Allen Collection)*

Above: The combination of the traditional West Riding green livery and the unfamiliar (in that livery) profile of the Bristol Lodekka was unusual and interesting. Ex-Midland General **10 DRB** (**478**), a 1957 58-seat LD6G model, was at Bank Street, Castleford, while working a local circular service. The vehicle joined the West Riding fleet in 1970 along with 49 more second-hand buses from sister NBC companies, and was withdrawn from service in 1972. *(David Allen Collection/L Pratt)*

Below: More modern in specification and with a higher seating capacity, and thus rather longer-lived in West Riding service, were **JAE 631/2D** (**547/8**), 1966 FLF Lodekkas, from the batch of 27 of this 70-seat front-entrance model that were brought in from the Bristol Omnibus Company. The buses are pictured at Belle Isle in NBC poppy-red livery and were withdrawn in 1979 and 1980 respectively. *(Geoff Coxon)*

Above: **KHL 655F** (**221**), from the 1967 intake of Roe-bodied Leyland Panthers, rests in Pontefract bus station in National Bus Company days. It had twelve years of service with West Riding.

Below: **PHL 245G** (**286**), a 1969 Plaxton-bodied 52-seat Bristol RELL6G, was also photographed, on the same day as the Panther above, in Pontefract. It was one of the first Bristols delivered after West Riding joined the National Bus Company in 1967. *(Both: Geoff Coxon)*

Above: **EWW 539Y** (**539**), a 1983 Leyland Olympian/ECW, makes its way out of Leeds to Castleford, where it was based. It clearly shows the contemporary British Bus style of livery. *(Andrew Jarosz)*

Below: **H338 UWT** (**338**), a 1990 Leyland Lynx 2 complete with red nose, at rest in Wakefield bus station. About this time Volvo was taking over Leyland and actually building the Lynx. The Volvo successor, the B10B model, included some design features from the Lynx. *(Malcolm King Collection/J C Leadbetter)*

Above: **L827 NYG (827)**, a 1993 Dennis Lance fitted with Alexander Strider bodywork, is seen in Kippax on the 163 Castleford to Leeds service. After the demise of the Leyland Lynx, a rethink on vehicle policy brought in a fleet of 30 Lances. Initial allocation was shared with Yorkshire Bus and eventually all were operated by the latter. *(Malcolm King)*

Below: Volvo B10B/Alexander Strider **K405 HWX (405)** of 1993 was the first of five delivered new to Selby and District and clearly shows the Caldaire Holdings livery styling adopted after West Riding became independent again in 1987. Further deliveries of this type for the main fleet followed in 1994. They featured double glazing which was somewhat of a luxury in an urban fleet. *(Andrew Jarosz)*

Above: **H710 UNW (710)**, a 1990 Optare MetroRider 23-seater, is shown working on a local service in Kirkgate, Wakefield.

Below: Dodge S56/Alexander 25-seater **E512 HHN (459)** of 1987 in Wakefield bus station. There was a requirement for larger buses than the Freight Rover Sherpas being used and Caldaire sister company United Automobile Services provided 21 of these Dodges. *(Both: Malcolm King Collection)*

Above: **L407 NUA** (**407**) is a 1993 Volvo B10B with Wright Endeavour bodywork. This was one of only four Wright-bodied buses among the flow of Volvo B10Bs arriving during this period, seating 49 for dual-purpose operation against the 51-seat service buses with Alexander Strider bodies. All four operated exclusively on the motorway services from Leeds and Bradford to Sheffield. *(John Senior)*

Below: **E52 TYG** (**52**), a 1988 Leyland Royal Tiger/Doyen 53-seat integral coach, was one of eight of these none-too-successful vehicles obtained for the joint coaching fleet established for the West Riding Group principally for those services taken over from National Express Rapide. *(Geoff Coxon)*

Above: **N623 KUA (623)**, a 1996 Volvo Olympian/Northern Counties seen in Piccadilly, York. This was one of three Olympians purchased for the Selby fleet, the first-double deckers obtained by West Riding for over 10 years. Note the top-deck tree-guard, an important protective measure for double-deck operations in rural areas. *(David Allen Collection)*

Below: **G332 NUM (332)**, a 1990 Leyland Lynx l is shown in its condition as delivered. A significant bus in the West Riding fleet: not only was it the last Lynx l to be delivered, it was also the last bus to operate in West Riding livery and was withdrawn as such in January 2002. It is fitting, therefore, that its image should be the last in this first West Riding volume. *(Andrew Jarosz)*